(Formerly titled, "The Point of Abuse")

I0158240

Red Flags

The Continuation of the Taquayasia Story

Yasmin S. Brown

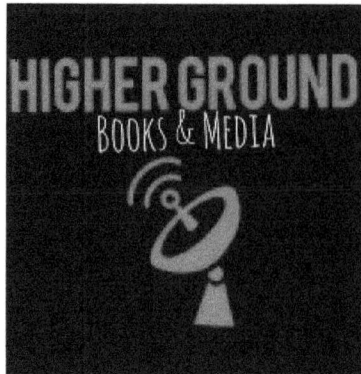

Higher Ground Books & Media
Springfield, Ohio.
http://highergroundbooksandmedia.com

Printed in the United States of America 2019

Yasmin S. Brown

TABLE OF CONTENTS

Yasmin S. Brown

Dedication

To women that have been in domestic situations and those that are not sure of the red flags. Love yourself first because without self-love you cannot love someone else. Staying in an unhealthy relationship that may cause you harm mentally, physically, or emotionally is never worth your life.

Yasmin S. Brown

Introduction

 Fresh out of high school living on her own Taquayasia
has put her past behind her and set a new outlook on
life. Getting ready to start college in August Taquayasia
is excited about her future. She moved out of her
mother's house into a messy entanglement.

Taquayasia meets a handsome gentleman name
TJ and goes through various love triangles and
relationship roller coasters which set her back
emotionally and mentally in life.

Yasmin S. Brown

Acquainted

Summer is in full swing Taquayasia is all grown up and out on her own. Moving into her own fully furnished apartment that she received for graduation from her parents. Taquayasia, Shonnese and her cousin Rashaunda are moving the last of the small items from her mother's house. Upon carrying the last of the boxes in the apartment; she stops and looks out the large sliding glass window. Taquayasia noticed a handsome, caramel colored, chiseled young man; whose six-pack abdominal muscles glisten as the sun touched his body. Taquayasia thought he was so appealing and sexy. Being shy and reserved Taquayasia just admired him from a distance since she was scared to say anything. A few days later Taquayasia and her sister, Shonnese, were on the porch enjoying the summer breeze when she told Shonnese about the deliciously chiseled fellow. While they were sitting there talking; out of the corner of Taquayasia's eye she noticed him on the steps of the apartment complex talking to his friends. Taquayasia shows her sister the physically fit young man as he stood with no shirt on; once again. Shonnese calls to the crowd of young men to get his attention. As Shonnese beckon him to come over Taquayasia becomes bashful. He introduced himself to Taquayasia and Shonnese as TJ; short for Anthony James. Taquayasia and TJ exchange numbers; that was the start of many conversations to come. They would confabulate on the

Yasmin S. Brown

telephone for hours, sharing their most intimate and sometimes disturbing secrets. Finally, after weeks of talking on the phone, Taquayasia invited TJ over. Once TJ arrived they stood in the hallway of the apartment building to have privacy since Shonnese was visiting. As they were talking Taquayasia starts to suffer a little light headed and dizzy sensation. Never telling TJ, she was feeling this way Taquayasia faints in the middle of their conversation and TJ quickly spring into action; taking Taquayasia back to her apartment. As Taquayasia older sister opens the door TJ tells her what happen. Shonnese tells TJ not to worry it happens sometimes when Taquayasia is dehydrated. Shonnese gives Taquayasia water and tells TJ she will be okay after resting. The next day TJ checks on Taquayasia to make sure she is okay. After dating TJ for about a year Taquayasia had no idea of the life-changing events that would soon change her outlook on ever dating again. TJ and Taquayasia began to discuss living together and starting a family. Taquayasia was on the fence about creating a family, but she thought he was a loving and caring person, because he showed concern for her when she fainted. She decided it would be nice to live and start a family with such a caring man. Their relationship was going great; dating and enjoying one another's company. Once TJ officially moved in he would pitch in with the bills, cooking and household chores. Taquayasia stop taking her birth control so they

Red Flags

can try to conceive to start their family. After six months of trying to conceive Taquayasia finally gets pregnant; excited and nervous all at once. Taquayasia waited a few days before telling TJ to make sure she really was pregnant. Their life was going to change forever which made Taquayasia feel scared. Taquayasia tells TJ while they are sitting in the living room watching bull riding. TJ was genuinely excited and her fear went away. Three months into the pregnancy TJ proposed to Taquayasia on Christmas day; Taquayasia accepts the proposal with extreme excitement. Her world is now going to take a 360-degree turn that she was not expecting from such a charismatic person.

Red Flags

Emotional Abuse

Repeated cheating with verbal abuse without sincerity of stopping the destructive behavior. This behavior breaks you down mentally and emotionally with no regards to your feelings.

Six months into the pregnancy Taquayasia has now started to show and all is well in their relationship. When one-day Taquayasia's best friend Steve came over to get his hair braided. Steve and Taquayasia had been best friends since high school. After Taquayasia finishes Steve's hair, something she had been doing for years, he left to go out with their mutual friends to a party. TJ was in the bedroom while Taquayasia braided Steve's hair. TJ didn't really like Steve but Taquayasia didn't know why. When Steve left TJ came out the bedroom yelling about her braiding Steve's hair. Taquayasia was confused because TJ knew she braided both men and women's hair all the time. TJ starts to tell Taquayasia she is fat and calls her a bitch then leaves. Crying and upset Taquayasia picks up the cordless house telephone, which sometimes intercepts other people's calls in her living quarters. Taquayasia proceed to call her sister, but what she overheard prior to dialing the number stopped her in her tracks. Taquayasia heard two women discussing one of them hooking up with this a guy that live in their complex. As she listened a little longer to one of the women giving a description of the man she discovered the guy they were speaking about was TJ. The woman spoke about details of hooking up with TJ on several occasions. Catching the voice of one of the women Taquayasia noticed it was her neighbor whose brother hung with TJ all the time. Confronting the neighbor, Sheree, Taquayasia asked her about the conversation she overheard. Sheree feeling uncomfortable with the conversation calls her dad to come speak with Taquayasia. Ralph, her neighbor's dad proceeds to tell Taquayasia they shouldn't get into an altercation over TJ's actions because they are related. Once they left Taquayasia sat and ponders on all the information she just took in. She decided to call her dad to find out if she and Sheree' were really related. Taquayasia's dad informs her that they are not really related but her grandmother helped to raise Ralph. After hanging up with her father Taquayasia waits for TJ to arrive at her house. TJ enters the house blindsided by the information Taquayasia discovered and he denies everything. Knowing TJ is lying Taquayasia puts him out of the house throwing his Jordan sneakers and engagement ring out the window. TJ moved in with his father that evening. The next day Taquayasia found out someone had stolen the sneakers. Upset and sad by the situation it did not bother her that someone had stolen the sneakers. Not understanding what she did wrong for TJ to step out on her, she cries. After a few months had gone by TJ called Taquayasia to try to work things out. Taquayasia accepts his apology and takes him back. TJ move back into the house with Taquayasia as they worked things out. The relationship seems to be going well as they prepared for their first child. Working on building trust back into their relationship

TJ and Taquayasia decide to attend Lamaze class. Once
they left Lamaze class one Spring day Taquayasia
received a telephone call from a female. The female
proceeds to tell Taquayasia she is with TJ at the jewelry
store. The female informed Taquayasia they got into an
argument and she can pick TJ up downtown.
Taquayasia hangs up with the female, then pages TJ; no
call back. A couple of hours went by when TJ walked in
the door. Questioning TJ about the telephone call, TJ
denies he was with the female. Taquayasia feels hurt all
over again because of TJ's cheating behavior. Without
any proof Taquayasia didn't know what to believe, so
she let it go. The next morning Taquayasia comes out
the house to get in the car when she noticed her tires
were slashed. Upset, she walked back into the house to
let TJ know what happen. TJ has the car towed down
the street to get the car fixed. At this point Taquayasia
becomes more suspicious of the telephone call from the
day before. TJ returns with the car to pick Taquayasia
up for Lamaze class. TJ leave out first and as
Taquayasia started to the door the telephone rings;
hello, the same female voice from the previous day
before, said, "I am waiting in the parking lot for TJ."
Seven months pregnant Taquayasia waddles outside to
the parking lot, passing her friends. Taquayasia's
friends asked where she is going; Taquayasia snapped,
"to the parking lot to see this female that keeps calling
my house." Walking fast, Taquayasia starts to get closer

to the parking lot. As she approaches TJ comes from the side apartment building. The girl was standing outside of her car with a pipe waiting for Taquayasia. TJ sees Taquayasia and runs over to stop her from approaching the girl. TJ finally gets Taquayasia back into the house and the female pulls off. Hot! Taquayasia start yelling at TJ. Taquayasia's friends hear her yelling outside and came to her apartment to calm her down, so she won't go into early labor. TJ left once Taquayasia's friends arrived. Taquayasia started to calm down after talking to her friends and telling them some of things she has been going through. Unfortunately, Taquayasia must put her feelings aside to attend Lamaze class with TJ. Sitting through class Taquayasia feels emotionally broken, but was not prepared for what happens after class. After class Taquayasia and TJ walk out of the building where the class was being held when the same car that was in the parking lot of her apartment complex hours before pulled up. The car that was in the parking lot stops next to Taquayasia and TJ and a female got out the car. The female and Taquayasia exchange words, then TJ got in the car with the female then drove off and left Taquayasia standing alone on the sidewalk. Upset, Taquayasia drove home packed TJ's clothes and threw them outside. A month goes by without speaking to TJ when the telephone rings, it's TJ. Trying to plead his case about his actions TJ apologized once again and stating he will never do it again. Accepting his apology once again, Taquayasia allows TJ to come visit. Bringing gifts TJ has weaken Taquayasia's wall she put up between them. Taquayasia takes TJ back again, but don't allow him to move back in. Approaching the due date Taquayasia start letting TJ stay over. During this night Taquayasia goes into labor while TJ was sleeping. Taquayasia punches TJ in the leg to wake him so they can drive to the hospital. With baby now here, things felt different between the couple. After all they've been through it made them closer. Now that the baby is here TJ comes over more often to help with duties as a father. Later in the year TJ and Taquayasia decided they are going to have date night for New Year's Eve. TJ invites his friend over to play Connect Four for shots. TJ has been getting a little possessive over Taquayasia since she had the baby. Since Taquayasia notice he was becoming possessive she thought having his friend come visit may change TJ's behavior. Laughing and drinking enjoying their get together with friends when out of nowhere TJ accuse Taquayasia of cheating. Taquayasia tries to tell him that is not true, but he didn't want to hear what she had to say. Puzzled TJ's friend remained silent. Whack! TJ smacks Taquayasia in front of his friend. Their relationship has gone from bad to worst.

Let's Talk

What are some of the red flags Taquayasia should have noticed?

_____

_____

_____

_____

_____

Do you think TJ's friend should have stepped into help Taquayasia?

_____

_____

_____

_____

_____

Intimidation, Control, Psychological, Verbal Abuses

Using intimidating language to control or create psychological fear. This behavior makes one feel worthless, incapable, and ashamed to seek help.

After TJ smack Taquayasia this left her feeling
sad, confused, and hurt of why he would do such a thing
to her. TJ and Brian left the house after what happen.
Crying, Taquayasia goes in her room and lays in the bed
holding her pillow. She Falls asleep after lying there for
some time. Taquayasia is waken by the telephone
ringing. Taquayasia gathers herself together to answer
the telephone, it's TJ. TJ apologize to Taquayasia for
putting his hands on her. Taquayasia accepted his
apology. Thinking it would be the first and last time he
hit her. Now back together, TJ and Taquayasia are
trying to work through their problems. Enjoying each
other and being a family is what Taquayasia always
wanted, minus the drama. One day, Taquayasia's friend
called to get his hair braided. She tells her friend it's
okay to come get his hair done, since she and TJ talked
about it the first time he came over. Before
Taquayasia's friend Brad arrived, TJ decided he was
going to leave, since he didn't like Brad. A few hours
later, Brad's hair was complete and TJ had returned. TJ
starts yelling at Taquayasia telling her that she and Brad
are having sex, then calling her a slut and whore. She
tries to tell him they are not sleeping together, but he is
not letting her get a word in. Taquayasia just listens to
TJ's rant because she didn't want him to hit her again.
TJ leaves and Taquayasia calls her sister Shonnese to
tell her what happen. Shonnese tells Taquayasia TJ is

crazy and she needs to leave him alone. Not heeding her sister's words Taquayasia stays with TJ. TJ never apologized about the incident and Taquayasia never brought it up out of fear. Sometime had gone by and Taquayasia and TJ are now getting back on the right track. Thanksgiving rolls around, TJ and Taquayasia goes to TJ's families house for the holiday. Everyone is nice and friendly, when TJ and his mother's husband get into an altercation. TJ's mother tries to calm him down, but it just made him angrier. We suddenly pack our family up in the car and proceed to leave. As we are driving off his mother and her husband come out on the porch when TJ stops the car, then goes in the trunk, pulls out a gun when his mother screams, NO! TJ lets off three shots in the air, POP! POP! POP! He gets back into the car and pulls off. Scared Taquayasia didn't breathe a word, it was a quiet car ride home with nothing, but the radio playing. TJ drop Taquayasia off at her apartment then drove off without a word. Later, the next evening TJ calls Taquayasia as if nothing happen. Not wanting to rock the boat Taquayasia goes along with the conversation. The next day she calls TJ to babysit, while she run errands; he agrees. A few hours went pass, no TJ. Still waiting, Taquayasia calls him at home, no answer. Frustrated Taquayasia starts to pack up the baby to come along with her to run errands when she noticed TJ outside of her window with his friends with a girl in his face. Taquayasia yells out the window; TJ ignored her. She yells again; he looks over. Walking toward her apartment she can see the anger on TJ's face. Not knowing what was going to take place when he came in the door; Taquayasia nervously awaited his arrival. TJ walks in the door and all hell breaks loose. He is yelling and swinging on Taquayasia, then Taquayasia attempts to defend herself when TJ pull out a gun and points it at her. Frozen, Taquayasia stands there stiff steering down the barrel of a gun fearing for her life when the patio door slides open. It's Taquayasia's cousin Greg. Greg lived in the same apartment complex as Taquayasia. Greg steps in front of Taquayasia telling TJ to lower his gun and if you shoot my cousin you will have to shoot me. Taquayasia is now standing behind Greg; TJ lowers the gun and leaves. The next sounds they hear are two gunshots. Pop! Pop! Jumping out of her frozen state after hearing the shots Taquayasia continue to pack up the baby thanks her cousin and goes to stay with her mother.

Yasmin S. Brown

Let's Talk

Should Taquayasia have stop being friends with
Brad to avoid conflict in her relationship?

_____

_____

_____

_____

Should Taquayasia have listen to Shonnese and
left TJ?

_____

_____

_____

_____

Physical Abuse

Hitting of any kind in aggressive behavior, using objects to beat, smothering, drowning and guns

This type of behavior grows from one incident to multiple and can lead to severe hospitalization or death.

Leaving the baby with her mother; Taquayasia returns home. Nervously thinking TJ may return she calls her friends from the apartment complex to come over. As Taquayasia and her friends are sitting in the living room talking; the telephone rings. Not wanting to answer the telephone; she answered anyway, hello. It is TJ's mother apologizing on TJ's behalf. After she apologized her tone changed; she sternly says, "I hope you're not going to keep the baby from us!" Sitting on the telephone in silence, Taquayasia did not know what to say. Replying with a soft, No. Once she hangs up the telephone her friends tell her maybe she should get PFA (protection against abuse) papers against TJ to be safe. Still feel scared and confused Taquayasia decide to go get the PFA papers. Taquayasia calls her sister to go with her to get the paperwork from the evening court. Taquayasia's friends left once Shonnese arrived to take her to court. As they arrived at court Taquayasia became scared of how TJ would react once he received the papers. The judge grants Taquayasia a temporary protection for 30 days and informs her she must go to family court to get a one-year protection. Taquayasia says okay, then she leaves to take the papers to the local police station. Giving the paperwork to the young tall and slender Caucasian officer who inform her he will be served the next day. A week goes by and Taquayasia goes back home with the baby. Starting to feel

Red Flags

comfortable in her home again she now tries to relax after everything. Now enjoying her life without coming home in fear. Taquayasia has a peace of mind. Around a month goes by when loneliness starts to set in; in addition to be a single parent. Taquayasia started to feel depressed about being a single mother as well as missing TJ; when the telephone rang. Hello, "Hi honey," TJ's mother states. I was calling you to get the baby, but those PFA papers you put on my son don't allow him to see the baby or you. Taquayasia apologize for the papers and keeping the baby away from them. She tells TJ's mother she will let them lapse for them to see the baby. The week after the PFA's lapse TJ's mother called again to ask if should can keep the baby for the weekend; Taquayasia says yes. Friday comes and Taquayasia drives over to TJ's mother's house, who happen to live in the same apartment complex as TJ, in Newark. Once Taquayasia arrives she noticed a familiar car, but did not think anything of it since they make more than one of the same cars. Taquayasia drops off the baby and head home. When Taquayasia gets home she put on her pajamas and turn on a Lifetime movie. Just wanting to rest from everything that has been going on Taquayasia dose off during the movie. Awaken the next morning by the telephone ringing, hello, it's TJ. We need to talk, he said. They decided co-parenting would be best for them right now, but as time went on they felt things between them were incomplete. TJ started to visit the baby more often and they would sit and reminisce on the good times between them. Enjoying the reminiscing Taquayasia starts to miss being with TJ. Utilizing Taquayasia's sensitivity to their memories TJ picked up on her body language. Taquayasia allowed him to talk her back in to his arms. Once TJ sealed the deal of getting back together with Taquayasia they hear a knock at the door; it TJ's friend. TJ leaves after telling Taquayasia he will talk to her later. Excited they are back together she leaves to pick up the baby. Once Taquayasia return from picking up the baby TJ comes back over. TJ is sitting on the couch holding the baby while they are watching bull riding like they use to do early in their relationship. TJ falls asleep holding the baby on his chest. Not wanting to disturb them Taquayasia placed a blanket on them and goes to bed. The next morning Taquayasia gets up to make breakfast. After breakfast TJ headed home. Taquayasia's head is now in the clouds with excitement of the reconciliation. Since they reunited TJ and Taquayasia spends a lot of time together or on the telephone while watching the same television program. Weeks went by and things were going great, then things started to change; less visit and calls. One hot summer day Taquayasia looked out the window and seen TJ getting into a black car in the parking lot of her apartment complex. Feeling confused on why TJ would be in her apartment complex without calling or visiting

Red Flags

her she pages him. Feeling sad she starts crying. Not again as the tears rolled down her face she fell for another apology. A couple of days went by without a call. When one Friday evening the telephone rang, hello; TJ is on the other end. Taquayasia asked if he was in her apartment complex the other day. TJ said, "I wasn't in your apartment complex the other day." Out of fear Taquayasia didn't want to force the issue, so she let it go. TJ ask if she can bring the baby on Saturday afternoon to his house. It's Saturday morning, Taquayasia is packing the baby's milk, clothes, shoes, and toys in the diaper bag to take over TJ's house. Taquayasia calls to tell TJ she is on her way. During the car ride Taquayasia starts to get an uneasy feeling about going to TJ's house. As the nervousness grew in her stomach she wondered why she felt so scared. As she pulls up she noticed a familiar car like the females. Not knowing who it belongs to she goes in to the building. Taquayasia proceeds up the steps to TJ's apartment. Taquayasia stop pass his Aunt Sheila's apartment to let her see the baby before she proceeded down the hallway to TJ's apartment. Sheila and Taquayasia walk down the hallway. As TJ open the door Taquayasia and Sheila walk in. While they are standing in the living room some female walks out of the backroom. Taquayasia catches a glimpse of the female. WOW, it's the same chick that came with a pipe to fight Taquayasia while she was seven months pregnant.

Yasmin S. Brown

Taquayasia snapped yelling at TJ and walking toward the female. TJ grabs Taquayasia then shoves her out the door. As Taquayasia is still yelling at the girl TJ shoves her again out the hallway door. As Taquayasia walks back in the hallway to go get the baby for Aunt Sheila TJ grabs her around the neck then starts choking her. TJ pushes Taquayasia by her neck back out the door leading to outside. Losing her footing and fall into a baby pool full of water sitting next to the hallway door. TJ gets on top of her and holds her head under the water. Fighting trying to get away Taquayasia starts to swallow water. Not knowing if she was going to live or die she hears a voice yelling get off her. It was Sheila and TJ's mother. TJ's mother takes Taquayasia and the baby back to her apartment upstairs from TJ's apartment. Scared, wet and nervous Taquayasia is shaking. TJ's mother attempts to calm Taquayasia down so she can drive home. Too scared to call the police Taquayasia gathers herself for the drive with the baby and never look back.

Let's Talk

Do you think Taquayasia should have kept the
PFA papers against TJ?

_____

_____

_____

_____

_____

Should someone have called the police after TJ
tried to drown Taquayasia?

_____

_____

_____

_____

_____

Patients of Love

The man most high, way up in the sky has created me in
his eye, not to stand for anything less than
unconditional love from above, not to get caught up in
turmoil that results in a push and a shove that's not
love, God wants us to be treated like a queen by some
who supports all our dreams even the ones that may fail
not to have us be locked up in a mental jail, A man of
that nature will not create an environment that causes
you the lack of self-love but show you the spiritual love
from above, now that is the patients of love.

Encouraging Words

Storms are temporary.

Believe in yourself because you are the child of the highest God.

God's grace gives you strength.

You have an essential purpose in this world.

You are beautiful and courageous.

Yasmin S. Brown

Help

National Domestic Violence Hotline

1-800-799-7233

Static Resource

DomesticViolenceStatistics.org/domestic-violence-statistics/

www.ingramcontent.com/pod-product-compliance
Lightning Source LLC
Chambersburg PA
CBHW021922040426
42448CB00007B/866